MANUSMRITI
THE
GREATEST KNOWLEDGE

Code of Social Conduct

RAM NIVAS KUMAR

MA (English), MLISc., MJMC, Dip-in-OA

Edition

2024
Copyright

Ram Nivas Kumar

PREFACE

It occurred to me high that a group of Hindu society is reeking with discontent in the matter of long prevailing caste system in India. Some people feel proud to be of the highest class and some are ashamed of being placed at the low. Hence, they must know the true fact of the caste system. They say—"The Manusmriti is the holy book that made their position low." So, we tried hard to let them know the actual position of all castes mentioned as Varnas in the Manusmriti. We have compiled the main teachings of the Manusmriti in a simple descriptive way.

Well, the Manusmriti in original is written in Sanskrit language in verses. We attempted to transcribe it in English in a simple and conversational language so that even a general student of English may get at the true meaning of the verses easily.

The book is written for the general learning of the facts mentioned in the Manusmriti. We picked out some most important and common teachings from all the twelve chapters of the Manusmriti in brief. It is meant for all people belonging to all strata of society of all castes and creeds. The contents written in this book are mere illustrative and not exhaustive.

Though, we took utmost care while translating into English, there may be minor differences in transliteration. For exact and the most accurate and elaborate meaning, readers are suggested to go with the original text wisely.

Readers, especially women and the downtrodden are requested to go through this book with open mind and unbiased thoughts in their interest. They are sure to get at the true meaning of the teachings.

Hope, the people at large would take more interest in reading this book and would try to understand the social structure at the time of origin of organized human race.

—*Ram Nivas Kumar*

 RAM NIVAS KUMAR

CONTENTS

1

INTRODUCTION

The Manusmriti is the laws of Manu. It is the most important religious book for the Hindus. It is to be followed by all Hindus irrespective of their castes or creeds. It is a law of all the social classes. The Manusmriti is believed to be the words of Brahma, the Lord. Maharaja Manu is the standpoint of reference for all future Dharmshastras that followed it. According to the Hindu tradition, the Manusmriti records the words of Brahma, the Supreme Creator. It is also called the *Manava Dharmshastra*. This Dharmshastra is a genre of Sanskrit text. It refers to the treatise (Shastra) on Hinduism. The textual corpus of Dharmshastra was composed in poetic verses. They are the parts of the Hindu Smritis.

WHO WAS MANU?

In Hindu mythology, *Shraddhadeva Manu* (Sanskrit—Manu Shraddhadeva) is the current Manu. He is the progenitor of the current humanity. In later texts, Manu is the title or name of mystical sage ruler of the earth, or alternatively the head of mystical dynasties that begin with each cyclic *Kalpa*(aeon) when the universe is born anew.

MEANING OF THE NAME MANU

Manu is a proper noun. He is the arch-type first man of Hindu methodology. He is the first survivor of the great flood. He is the Father of the human race. He is also a legendary author of one of the most famous Codes of Hindu Religious Law, the Manusmriti (Laws of Manu). This law is composed in Sanskrit in poetic verses.

MEANING OF MAN AND MANUAL

The Latin root word "man" means "hand." This root word is the origin of a number of English vocabulary words including manuscript, manufacture and manicure. It is easy to remember that "Man" means "hand". The word "manual" is through the root word "man" which is an adjective that describes a "task done by hand."

The Manusmriti translated as the "Laws of Manu" or the "Institutions of Manu" is the most important and authoritative Hindu

Law Book (Dharmshastra) which served as a foundation work on Hindu law and Jurisprudence in ancient India. Until the modern times, it was the standard reference for adjudicating civil and criminal cases by both the rulers who patronized Vedic faith and the people who practised Hinduism. Hinduism has many law books. Of them, the Manusmriti is certainly the most popular and authoritative work.

Manu in Hindu tradition is considered to be the first of Brahma's son. He is considered progenitor of human race. Therefore, it is difficult to determine the age of the Manusmriti. The laws of Manu might have been known to the Vedic people for long time before they were codified into their present form. The work that we have today as "The Manusmriti" might have reached its final form thousands of years ago.

The people of ancient India believed in the order and regulation of the world as the manifestation of God's will and intent. They believe in the clear victory of the divine forces over the demonic. Hence, the laws governing the conduct of individual and regulating the Hindu society were formulated by many scholars and sages in ancient India since the earliest time. Their works are today available to us as *Dharmshastras,* of which the work of Manu (The Manusmriti) is considered the most important and widely used.

Unlike the Vedas, the Hindu law books fall into the category of intellectual or scholarly works (Smritis). They are distilled and codified through observation, experience, analysis, and the study of the Vedas keeping in view the best interest of the humanities and society. However, they are not entirely free from the flaws of humans. They are also not free from castes or racial bias. Hence, they are vulnerable to criticism from the modern standpoint.

The Manusmriti projects an ideal society. It projects ideal human conduct. It gives the ideal base to establish an orderly society. It teaches us to lead a divine centred and happy life. To promote these ideals and enforce divine will, it proposes numerous laws to minutely govern human life and conduct as applicable to their social classes, duties and responsibilities. Its purpose is to inculcate discipline in people. It provides a basis for the rulers to enforce lawful conduct. It ensures the order in progression of the world through righteous conduct and observation of obligatory duties by individuals who have chosen for themselves the life of a householder or that of a renouncing.

The power to enforce the laws is carefully distributed among the rulers and the guardians of society who assist the king in decision making. The Manusmriti recognizes the corrupting and deluding influence of power over the mind. It cautions the king to exercise his judgement with great care to avoid sinful *karma* and harmful consequences for him and for the world.

The laws that were proposed by Manu to govern human conduct and society reflect the conditions, needs and values of the times in which they were formulated. Some of them do not fit into the present day value system. They acknowledge prevailing social and gender inequality as natural conditions of human existence. They propose laws to govern the behaviour of individuals without providing scope for any change that time may bring in the conditions of society or the lives of people. Hence, today we may find some laws archaic, outdated and even primitive.

The laws (The Manusmriti) favour a paternalistic society and family system vesting the authority to regulate them with men and proposing rather a subordinate status and subservient role to women. They also betray a clear lack of thrust in the integrity and sexual choices of women. Thereby, they (the laws) suggest that they (women) should always be guarded by men and should never be left alone in the presence of men outside their families. They undermine the role of woman in family and domestic matters. They urge men to treat them with honour and respect and not let them suffer.

The British who ruled India used the Manusmriti as the standard to settle disputes among Hindus with regard to matters of inheritance, family disputes, marriage and royal succession. Some Hindu scholars believe that the British found in the Manusmriti a useful tool to promote their interest or perpetuate the society divide among the Hindus to consider their power. There is also a criticism that for a long time, the Manusmriti serves the interests of the privileged classes and justifies the oppression of women and the lower castes, as they prescribe unequal laws for different castes based upon the status in society.

The Manusmriti acknowledges and justifies the caste system as the basis of order and regularity of society. It clearly recognises four classes of people—Brahmans, Kshatriyas, Vaishyas and Shudras and their respective roles in the preservation of Dharma.

People say that Brahmans and Kshatriyas are given many privileges and great leniency in matters of punishment for misconduct while Shudras are given the least number of privileges but the harshest of punishments even for minor misdemeanours. Hence, it is important to study the Manusmriti with an open mind to understand the actual facts. It is also necessary to know its historical and religious significance in the evolution of Hinduism from its early days to its present form.

It is difficult to apply the laws of Manu in today's world since the conditions that exist are very different from those when they were formerly codified. For example, our current laws do not permit gender bias or the imposition of restrictive laws upon women and their freedom to chase their marriage partners, their professions or their ways of life. Similarly, the laws governing the conduct of people according to their caste or occupation are discriminatory by today's standards and cannot be enforced. Despite such problems and limitations, the Manusmriti has high historical values. Students of Hinduism immensely need to study it to understand the way of life in ancient India. They need to know how people governed their lives with this law.

2
STRUCTUREOF THE MANUSMRITI

The Vedas are the most sacred scriptures of the Hindus. They constitute the most identical work which every Hindu tradition and sect claims as its source. They also embody the most vital rituals of the world. The Vedas are not man-made. They are self-existent. So as is the Manusmriti.

The Manusmriti is the most pious book of the Hindus. The version of the Text of the Manusmriti is sub-divided into twelve *Adhyayas* (chapters). The Text can be broadly divided into four, each of them is of different length and each further divided into sub sections:

1. Creation of the world
2. Sources of Dharma
3. Dharma of the four social classes
4. Laws of karma, rebirth and final liberation.

The Text is composed of in metric *Shlokas* (verses) in the form of dialogue between an exalted teacher and disciples who are eager to learn about the various aspects of Dharma. The *Sarvasva Sambhav* (origin, creation of the world) section has one hundred and nineteen verses describing how the world was created out of complete darkness, the cosmic energy, the cyclic nature of time and all existence.

MANUSMRITI OUTSIDE INDIA

The Dharmshastra, particularly the Manusmriti, states Anthony Reid, was greatly honoured in Burma (Myanmar), Sri Lanka, Thailand, Cambodia and Java-Bali (Indonesia) as the defining documents of the natural order which Kings were obliged to uphold. They were copied, translated and incorporated into law code with strict adherence to the original text in Burma and Sri Lanka and a stronger tendency to adapt to local needs in Java (Indonesia).

The Manusmriti is the first book written on the law in the whole world which deals with social and moral conduct of a person. The Manusmriti falls in the Smriti category of the Hindu scriptures. It is not less authoritative than the Vedas and the Upanishads. The Manusmriti is also known as Dharmshastra of Manav. There are other Smritis also like NaradSmriti, YajnavalkayaSmriti, BrihaspatiSmriti, etc. But the Manusmriti is the most famous of all them.

The Manusmriti does not talk about caste. But it talks about Varna, viz. Brahman, Kshatriya, Vaishya, and Shudra. There is no mention of Varna according to birth. But it advocates the system based on the qualities of a person. If a Shudra possesses the quality of a Brahmin, he could be promoted as a Brahmin. But if a Brahmin does not possess the qualities required, then he could be demoted as a Shudra.

The whole Veda is the first source of 'sacred law', next the tradition and the virtuous conduct of those who know the Veda. Further, also the customs of holy men and finally, self-satisfaction are the sources of 'sacred law.'

Whatever law has been ordained for any person by many, that has been fully declared in the Veda. Learn that sacred law which is followed by men learned and assented to in the hearts by the virtuous, even exempt from hatred and inordinate affection.

3
ALL THE FOUR VEDAS

RIG VEDA

The Rig Veda is the oldest and the most important of all the Vedas. It has richly contributed to other Vedas. Its hymns are called ricks. The Rig Veda is an important source of Vedic history. It contains many important hymns, such as PurushaSukta and Creation Hymns. The Rig Veda is an ancient collection of Vedic Sanskrit hymns along with associated commentaries on liturgy, ritual and mystical exegesis. It is one of the four canonical sacred texts (Shruti) of Hinduism known as the Vedas.

The core text of the Rig Veda Samhita, is a collection of 1028 hymns (Suktas) in about 10,600 verses organised into ten books. The book is composed of with hymns. They are mostly praise of specific deities. Some deal with philosophical or speculative questions. Some deal with the virtue of *Dana* (charity) in society.

The Rig Veda is the largest of the four Vedas. Many of its Verses appear in the other Vedas. Almost all the verses found in the Sama Veda are taken from different parts of the Rig Veda either once or as repetition.

SAMA VEDA

The Sama Veda is the Veda of melodious chants. It is an ancient Vedic religious text in Sanskrit. It is an important part of the Vedic scripture of Hinduism. Sama Veda, one of the four Vedas, is a liturgical text which consists of 1875 verses. All but 75 verses have been taken from Rig Veda.

Embodied inside the Sama Veda are the widely studied *Chhandogya Upanishada* and *Kena Upanishada* considered as the primary Upanishadas. The classical Indian music and dance tradition consider the chants and melodies in Sama Veda as one of its roots. It is also referred to as Sama Veda. The Sama Veda Samhita is not meant to be read as a text. It is like a musical score sheet that must be heard. The text uses creative structures to help embellish, transform or play with the words so that they stand fit into a desired musical harmony. The contents of the

Sama Veda represent a tradition and creative synthesis of music, sounds and spirituality.

The Sama Veda is the second most important Veda. It carries great significance in ritual singing because of its musical and lyrical quality. Its hymns are known as *Sammons* sung in specific meters.

YAJUR VEDA

The Yajur Veda meaning prose mantra and Vedic knowledge is the Veda of prose mantras. It is an ancient Vedic Sanskrit text. It is a compilation of ritual offering formulas that were said by a priest while an individual performed ritual actions such as those before the *yagna*. The Yajur Veda is one of the four Vedas and one of the scriptures of Hinduism. The exact century of the Yajurveda's composition is unknown. It is estimated by scholars to be on ground 1200 to 1000 BC, contemporaneous with the Sama Veda and the Atharva Veda.

The earliest and the most ancient layer of the Yajur Veda Samhita includes about 1875 verses. They are said to be laid upon the foundation of verses in the Rig Veda. The middle layer includes the *Satapatha Brahman,* one of the largest Brahman Texts in the Vedic collection. The youngest layer of the Yajur Veda Text includes the largest collection of primary Upanishadas. These include the *Brihadaranya Upanishada,* the *Isha Upanishada,* the *Taittriya Upanishada,* the *Katha Upanishada* and *the Maitriya Upanishada.*

The Yajur Veda says: God is Supreme. It has no Pratima (idol). It has no material shape. He cannot be seen directly by anyone. He pervades all beings and all directions. Thus, idolatry does not find any support from the Vedas.

ATHARVA VEDA

The Atharva Veda is the knowledge storehouse of atharvans, the procedures for everybody's life. The text is the fourth Veda. It has been a late addition to the Vedic scriptures of Hinduism.

The Atharva Veda is composed of in Vedic Sanskrit. It is a collection of 730 hymns with about 6000 mantras. About one sixth of the Atharva

Veda text adopts verses from the Rig Veda. The text is in poetry form deploying a diversity of Vedic matters.

In contrast to the liturgical religion of the other three Vedas, the Atharva Veda is said to represent a popular religion. Formulas for daily rituals are incorporated. Royal rituals and the duties of the court-priests are also included in the Atharva Veda.

The Atharva Veda was likely compiled as a Veda contemporaneously with the Sama Veda and the Yajur Veda. Along with the Samhita layer of the text, the Atharva Veda includes a Brahmans text. Final layer of the text covers philosophical speculations. The latter layer of Atharva Veda Text includes three primary Upanishadas influential to various schools of Hindu philosophy. These include the *Mundaka Upanishada*, the *Mandukya Upanishada* and the *Prashna Upanishada*.

The Atharva Veda is the most recent of the Vedas quartet. For a long time, it was not even considered a Veda. It contains mostly marital rituals to cast charms. It seeks protection against death and diseases. It attracts lovers. It causes to prevent harm. The Vedas essays are difficult to understand since they contain a lot of symbolism and archaic expressions. These essays may help you increase your knowledge of the Vedas, Vedic philosophy, beliefs and practices. It gives knowledge of Vedic rituals and sacrifices, mantras, Vedic gods and Vedic goddesses.

UPANISHADAS

Upanishads are the end parts of the Vedas. They contain gems of spiritual wisdom. They constitute the heart of Hindu philosophical enquiry and exploration of essentials. They are ancient Sanskrit texts that contain some of the central philosophical concepts and ideas of Hinduism, some of which are shared with religious traditions like Buddhism and Jainism.

BRAHMANA

If Atman is the lord of the body; Brahman is the lord of the Universe. He is the eternal, indestructible, all paradigms, supreme self and synonymous with the Vedas themselves. The Vedas contain the hidden power of Brahman in sound. It forms the indestructible knowledge (*Akshara*).

ATMANA

Atman means the breathing one, the individual soul. According to the Vedic beliefs, it is without form and without attributes. It is usually referred to as a Self. Atmana is the deity in our body extolled in classical yoga as *Ishavara,* the Lord.

VEDANTA

Vedanta means the end of the Vedas which is referred to the Upanishads and the knowledge they contain. Vedanta deals with essential truths as the source of existence, the nature and process of creation, the nature of reality, mortality, delusion, bondage, and liberation as souls from *samsara.*

BHAGAVADGITA

Bhagavadgita means song of God and the song for the servants of God. It is the simplified, condensed and summarized version of the Vedas. It is in a conversational or dialogue form for easy understanding and practice.

VEDIC PANTHEON

Not many people know that in the Vedic cosmology all beings are imitations so that no class of beings become supreme, powerful and upset the balance of creation. God defends humans against floods. Human depends upon gods for their peace and prosperity.

HISTORY

Vedic people kept their knowledge secret and maintained no historical records. The tradition continued in India for over 5000 years. As a result, it is difficult to construct Indian history and understand the historical process that shaped Hinduism.

CODE OF CONDUCT

One of the distinguishing features of Vedic civilization was the Smriti. Literature, especially the body of knowledge contained in the law books or book of duties are known as Dharmshastras.

The knowledge of the sacred Law is prescribed for those who are not given to the acquisition of the weak. The knowledge of the sacred Law is prescribed for those who are not given to the gratification of their desires. It is for those who seek the knowledge of the sacred Laws like this:

The Agnihotra sacrifice may be optionally performed at any time after the sun has risen.

A Brahman is purified by water that reaches his heart. A Kshatriya is purified by water that reaches his throat. A Vaishya is purified by water taken into his mouth and a Shudra is purified by water touched with the extremity of his lips.

At the beginning and at the end of the Veda's study, he must always clasp his both hands joining and he must clasp the feet of his Guru joining his hands.

The mono-syllable (Om) is the highest Brahman. Three suppressions of the breath are the best form of austerity.

Maternal aunt, paternal aunt and mother-in-law must be honoured like the wife of one's teacher. They are equal to the wife of one's teacher.

A learned man after fully scrutinising with the eye of knowledge should be intent on his duties.

For, that man who obeys the law prescribed in the revealed Texts in the sacred tradition gains fame in this world and after death unsurpassable bliss.

The ceremony called *Kesant* is ordained for a Brahman in the sixteenth year from conception. The ceremony called *Kesant* for a Kshatriya is ordained in the twenty-second year. And the ceremony called *Kesant* for a Vaishya is ordained two years later than that.

The whole series of ceremonies must be performed for females also in order to sanctify the body at the proper time and in the proper order.

With crossed hands, he must clasp the feet of the teacher. He must touch the left foot with his left hand and the right foot with his right hand.

Always pronounce the syllable 'Om' at the beginning and at the end of a lesson in the Veda. Unless the syllable 'Om' precedes the lesson, it will slip away from him and unless it (Om) follows, it (lesson) will fade away.

In the eighth year after conception, one should perform the initiation (Upanayana) of a Brahman. In the eleventh year after conception, one should perform the initiation (Upanayana) of a Kshatriya. But in the twelfth year after conception, one should perform the initiation (Upanayana) of a Vaishya. There is no mention of initiation (Upanayana) for the Shudras. Shudras need not initialise Upanayana as the Smriti is silent here.

The initiation of a Brahman who desires proficiency in sacred learning should take place in the fifth year after conception. The initiation (Upanayana) of a Kshatriya who wishes to become powerful should take place in the seventh year after conception. And the initiation of a Vaishya who long for success in his business should take place in the eighth year after conception.

The time for the savitri (initiation) of a Brahman does not pass until the completion of the sixteenth year after conception. The time for the savitri (initiation) of a Kshatriya does not pass until the completion of the twenty-second. And, the time for the savitri (initiation) of a Vaishya does not pass until the completion of the twenty-fourth.

Food, that is always worshipped, gives strength and manly vigour. But if eaten in excess, it destroys them both. Excessive eating is prejudicial to health. It is prejudicial to bliss in heaven. Excessive eating prevents spiritual merit. It is odious. One ought to avoid it carefully.

Let him not give to any man what he leaves. Left-over is not to be eaten by any person. Even husband and wife must not eat from the same vessel. And beware of eating between the two meal times. Let him not overeat. Let him not go anywhere without purifying himself after his meal.

4

UNTOUCHABLE CASTES AND VARNA SYSTEM

The Vedic text neither mentions the concept of untouchable people nor any practice of untouchability. The rituals in the Vedic text ask the noble or king to eat with the commoner.

The post Vedic text particularly the Manusmriti mentions outcastes and suggests that they be ostracized. The Vedic literature *Dharma Shutras* and *Dharmshastras* do not support the practice of untouchability at all.

VARNA

Varna is a Sanskrit word which means type, order, colour or class. The term refers to the social class in Brahminical books like the Manusmriti. The Manusmriti and other Hindu literature classified the society in primitive line into four Varnas:

Brahman—priests, scholars, teachers.

Kshatriya—rulers, warriors, administrators.

Vaishya—agriculturists and merchants.

Shudras—labourers and service providers.

SAVARNA

Communities which belong to one of the four Varnas or classes are called Savarna. In the present day context, they include all the forward castes. The Dalits and the Scheduled Tribes who do not belong to any Varnas are Avarna. Avarna in the Sanskrit language means one who does not have a Varna. The term denotes those sections of people in the Hindu text who do not belong to the four major Varnas, such as Scheduled Castes and Scheduled Tribes.

Brahman is a Varna (class) in Hinduism specializing as priests, teachers, *acharyas* and protectors of sacred learning across generations. The traditional occupation of Brahman was that of priesthood at the Hindu temple. Socio-religious ceremonies and rites of passage rituals, such as solemnising a wedding with hymns and prayers were his professions. Theoretically, the Brahmans were at the highest ranking of the four social classes. The texts suggest that Brahmans were agriculturists, warriors, traders and have held the variety of other occupations in India.

KSHATRIYA

kshatriya is one of the four Varnas of the Hindu society. The Sanskrit term kshatriya is used in the context of Vedic society wherein members organized themselves into four classes—Brahman, Kshatriya, Vaishya and Shudra. Traditionally, the Kshatriyas constitute the ruling and military elite. Their role was to protect society by fighting in wartime and governing in peacetime.

SHUDRA

Shudra is a Varna (class/caste) in Hinduism. Various sources translate it into English as a caste or as a social class. It is the lowest rank of the Varnas.

The word 'shudra' appears in the Rig Veda. It is also found in other Hindu texts, such as the Manusmriti, Arthashastra, Dharmshatras, Bhagavadgita, etc. Theoretically, Shudras constitute the hereditary labouring class serving others. It is really they have shared occupations with other Varnas including traders or warriors. In some cases, they participated in the carnation of kings. They were ministers and kings as well accordingly to early Indian texts.

The Shudras are not required to learn the Vedas. They are not twice-born (Dvij). Their occupational sphere started as service (seva) of the other three Varnas. Though, the word 'Dvij' is neither found in any Vedas and Upanishads nor it is found in any Vedang literature.

The traditional occupation of Shudra is described as labourers and service providers. The Arthashastras mentions Shudras as artisan. Theoretically, the position of the Shudras was very low. But there is evidence to show that many of them were well-to-do. Some of them succeeded in marrying their daughters in royal families. Sumitra, one of the four wives of the king Dasharatha, was a Shudra. Some of them even worked their way up to throne. The farmer Chandragupta is traditionally known to be a Shudra.

Among the Hindu communities of Bali in Indonesia, the Shudras have typically been the temple priests. Temple priest may also be a Brahman, Kshatriya or Vaishya. In most regions, it has been the Shudras who typically make offerings to the gods on behalf of the Hindu devotees. They chant prayers, recite Vedas and set the course of Balinese temple services. One states that Shudras are the bravest, other states that Shudras are the purest.

Richard Eaton, a professor of History, writes—"Anyone could become a warrior regardless of social origin. Nor the Jati appears as feature of people's identity. Occupations were fluid." Evidence shows, according to Eaton, that Shudras were part of the nobility. And many fathers and sons of different professions suggest that social status was earned, not inherited in the Hindu population.

Historical evidences left by Buddhist rulers in ancient and medieval India do not mention Shudra. For example, according to Johannes Bronkhorst, none of Ashoka's inscriptions mention the terms Kshatriya, Vaishyas or Shudras. They only mention Brahmins.

The caste system in India is the paradigmatic ethnographic example of caste. This has origins in ancient India and was transformed by various ruling elites in the medieval, early modern and modern India, especially in the Mughal Empire and the British Raj. It is today the basis of educational and job reservations in India which, a majority of people say, is eating into the vitality of the nation. It consists of two different concepts—Varna and Jati, which may be regardless as different levels of analysis of this system.

The system, as it exists today, is thought to be the result of developments during the collapse of the Mughal era and the British colonial regime in India. The collapse of the Mughal era saw the rise of the powerful who associated themselves with kings and priests. It also reshaped many casteless social groups into differentiated caste communities. The British Raj furthered this development making rigid caste organization a central mechanism of administration. Between 1860 and 1920 the Britishers segregated Indians by castes granting administrative jobs and senior appointments only to the upper castes. Social unrest during the 1920s led to a change in this policy. From then on, the colonial administration has a policy of positive discrimination by reserving a certain percentage of government jobs for the lower castes.

The Manusmriti was one of the first Sanskrit texts studied by the British. It was first translated into English by Sir William Jones. His version was published in 1794. It is also known as *Manava Dharmshastra* at the most. According to the Hindu tradition, the Manusmriti records the words of Brahma by attributing the words to supernatural forces. The Text takes on an authoritative tone as a Statement on Dharma. The Manusmriti is written with a focus on the "Shoulds" of Dharma rather than on the actuality of every day practice in India. At the present time, its practical application should not be underestimated.

HINDUISM

Hinduism is an Indian religion. It is the religion of the Hindus. It is the Dharma of the humans. It is a way of life widely practiced in the Indian sub-continent. Hindu has been called the oldest religion in the world. Some practitioners and scholars refer to it as *Sanatana Dharma.* This is an eternal tradition or the alter way beyond human history. Scholars regard Hinduism as a fusion or synthesis of various cultures and traditions with diverse roots.

Hinduism is the largest religion in India with at least 75% of the population identifying themselves as Hindus. Hinduism is considered to be the successor of Vedic religion. Hinduism is the religion of the majority of people in India and Nepal. It also exists among significant population outside the sub-continent. It has over 900 million adherents worldwide.

Hinduism contains a broad range of philosophies linked by shared concepts, recognisable rituals, cosmology, shared textual resources and pilgrimage to sacred rites. Hindu texts are classified into Shruti (heard) and Smriti (remembered). These texts discuss theology, philosophy, mythology, Vedic yajna, yoga, yajnamic rituals, and temple building. Sources of authority and eternal truths in its texts play an important role.

Prominent theme in Hindu beliefs includes the four *purusharthas*. The proper goals or aims of human life are Dharma (ethics/duties), Artha (prosperity/work), Karma (desire/passion) and Moksha (liberation/freedom/salvation).

WHO WERE THE SHUDRAS?

There is a book namely "Who Were The Shudra?" It is a history book written by Indian social reformer, Dr. Bhim Rao Ambedkar. The book discusses the origin of the Shudra Varna. Dr. Ambedkar says: Shudras were originally Aryans. They were a part of Kshatriya Varna belonging to the Solar race (Suryavansha). Dr. Ambedkar writes in the preface of the book—"Undoubtedly, the conclusion which I have reached as a result of my investigations is that the Shudras were one of the Aryan communities of the Solar race." The Shudras are at the lowest rank of the four Varna in which Indian society was traditionally divided. But they are definitely higher in rank than the untouchable, a category so demeaned in state that it is not even referred to in the classical Varna model.

ARE DALITS AND SHUDRAS THE SAME?

Though, Shudras were beneath the other Varnas and supposed to serve them, they were not untouchables and could even enter the temple and on so. The word "shudras" originally belonged to a tribe in the Vedic period. Untouchables are lowest rung of Shudras. They are more like prisoners of war enslaved for doing the lowest of jobs. Some of these untouchables slowly became outsiders breaking free from the Brahminical society.

Dalit is a common name given to the untouchables, Scheduled Castes and Scheduled Tribes. Actually, Scheduled Castes and Scheduled tribes were never untouchables. They were simple. But they were outside the fold of the Dhamshastras. Meaning, they do not even belong to the culture or religion of people who formed Varnas and Jatis in Dhamashastras.

The people of ancient India believed in the order and regularity of the world. They believe in the manifestation of God's will and intent. They believe in the clear victory of the divine force. Hence, the laws governing the conduct of individual and the order and regularity of Hindu society were formulated by many scholars and sages in ancient India. They also believe the Manusmriti as the order of the supreme soul, the Lord.

5
TEACHINGS OF THEMANUSMRITI

CHAPTER I

Since the Manusmriti is the most important to understand the historical progress of Hinduism and Hindu society, we have brought to you the translation of some most important parts of the Scripture (Text) in short which you can access from the following:

The universe existed in the shape of darkness, unperceived, destitute of distinctive marks, unattainable by reasoning unknowable, as if it were in deep sleep.

Then, the divine self-existent (Svayambhu Himself) appeared with irresistible creative power and created all living creatures and dispelled the darkness.

The Self-existent (the Supreme Creator) is subtle, indiscernible, and eternal. He created all living beings. He is inconceivable, shone forth of His own will.

In order to distinguish actions, He separated merit from demerit. He caused the creatures to be affected by the pairs of opposites such as pain and pleasure.

But to whatever course of action, the Lord, at first, appointed the king to govern all beings.

For the sake of the prosperity of the world, He caused the Brahman, the Kshatriya, the Vaishaya and the Shudra to proceed from His mouth, from His arms, from His thighs and from His feet. Dividing His own body, the Lord became half male and half female.

O most holy among twice-born! Know Me to be the Creator of this whole world.

In order to protect this universe, He, the most resplendent One, assigned separate occupations to those which sprang from His mouth, arms, thighs and feet.

He assigned the Brahmans to study and teach the Veda sacrificing their own benefits. He assigned them to receive the alms.

He commanded the Kshatriya to protect the people, to bestow gifts, to offer sacrifices, to study the Veda and to abstain from attaching themselves to sensual pleasures.

He ordered the Vaishya to tend cattle, to bestow gifts, to offer sacrifices, to study the Veda, to trade, to lend money and to cultivate land.

The Lord prescribed only one occupation for the Shudra, i.e. to serve meekly all the three castes.

The Brahma declared the mouth to be the purest part. As a Brahman sprang from His mouth, as he was the first born, and as he possesses the knowledge of the Veda, he is by right the lord of this whole creation. The very birth of a Brahman is an eternal incarnation. He is born to fulfil the sacred law.

A Brahman is born as the highest on the earth. He is the lord of all created beings. He is the protector of the treasury of the sacred law. On account of the excellence of the origin of the Brahman, he is entitled to all. He sanctifies any company which he enters.

A twice-born man who possesses regard for the most should be always careful about it.

Women must be honoured and adorned by their fathers, brothers, husbands and brothers-in-law who desire welfare.

A Kshatriya who has received the sacrament prescribed by the Veda, must duly protect this whole world.

The Lord created the King for the protection of the whole creation. A King is formed of the particles of gods. He, therefore, surpasses all created beings in lustre.

The Manusmriti recommends non-violence towards everyone and temperance as key virtues. All the four Varnas must abstain from injuring any creature. They must abstain from falsehood and must abstain from appropriating property of others.

Whatever exists in the world is the property of the Brahman on account of the excellence of his origin. A Brahman eats but his own food, wears but his own apparel, bestows but his own alms. Other mortals subsist through the benevolence of the Brahman.

A learned Brahman must carefully study everything and he must instruct his pupils. The rule of conduct is a transcendent law. A Brahman who departs from the rule of conduct does not reap the fruits of the Veda. But a Brahman who follows it will obtain the full reward.

TEACHINGS OF THE MANUSMRITI

CHAPTER II

The Manusmriti gives the learning of recommended virtues to compassion, forbearance, faithfulness, non-injury, self-control, non-desiring, mediation, serenity, sweetness and honesty which every person must learn and practice. Sacred Law is followed by men, the learned. Sacred Law is assented to in their hearts by the virtuous. The virtuous are ever exempt from hatred and inordinate affection. Just learn like this:

To act solely from a desire for reward is not laudable.

The whole Veda is the first source of the sacred law, next the tradition and the virtuous conduct of those who know the Veda.

Let the first part of a Brahman's name denote something auspicious. A kshatriya's name should be connected with power. And a Vaishya's name should be connected with wealth. But a Shudra's name should express contemptible.

The second part of a Brahman's name shall be a word implying happiness. The second part of a Kshatriya's name shall be a word implying protection. The second part of a Vaishya's name shall be a term expressing thriving. And, the second part of a Shudra's name should be an expression denoting service.

The name of woman should be easy to pronounce. It should not imply anything dreadful. Her name should possess a plain meaning. Her name should be pleasing and auspicious. Her name should end in long vowel. It should contain a word of benediction.

A sacrificial string (janaeu) of a Brahman shall be made of cotton twisted to the right consisting of three threads. A sacrificial string (janaeu) of a kshatriya shall be made of hempen threads, and the sacrificial string (janaeu) of a Vaishya shall be made of woollen threads.

A Brahman is purified by water that reaches his heart. A Kshatriya is purified by water reaching his throat. A Vaishya is purified by water taken into his mouth. And, a Shudra is purified by water touched with the extremity of his lips.

A Brahman is he who is learned in the Vedas.

The Brahman, the Kshatriya, and the Vaishya who neglect the performance of the rites prescribed for them will be blamed among virtuous men.

The monosyllable 'Om' is the highest Brahman. Three suppressions of the pious word 'Om' at the breath are the best form of austerity.

Desire is never extinguished by the enjoyment of desired objects. It only grows stronger like a fire.

Through the attachment of his organs to sensual pleasure, a man undoubtedly will incur guilt. But if he keeps them under complete control, he will obtain success in winning all his aims.

If a man keeps all the ten organs as well as the mind in subjection, he may gain all his aims.

One must not sit down on a couch, or on the seat which a superior occupies.

A Brahman, who does not know the form of returning a salutation, must not be saluted by a learned man.

Know that a Brahman of ten years and a Kshatriya of one hundred years stand to each other in the relation of father and son. Between those, the Brahman is the father.

The teacher is ten times more venerable than a sub-teacher. The father is a hundred times more venerable than the teacher. But the mother is a thousand times venerable than the father.

Of him who gives natural birth, and of him who gives the knowledge of the Vedas, the giver of the knowledge of the Veda is more venerable than father.

Seniority of Brahmans is from sacred knowledge. The seniority of a Kshatriya is from valour. The seniority of a Vaishya is from wealth in gain. But the seniority of a Shudra is from the age. According to the great sages—Atri and Gautama, he, who weds a Shudra woman, becomes an outcast.

A Brahman who takes a Shudra wife to his bed will sink into hell. If he begets a child by her, he will lose the rank of a Brahman.

Woman must be honoured and adorned by their father, brother, husband and brother-in-law.

One must not consider him a guest who dwells in the same village.

A guest reaches at the time of sunset must not be driven away by the house-holder.

A guest must not stay at a house if it lacks entertainment.

A Kshatriya, who comes to the house of a Brahman, is not called a guest. Nor a Vaishya, nor a Shudra, nor a personal friend or a relative, nor a teacher should be considered as a guest if comes to the house of a Brahman.

After the Brahman's kinsmen and the servants have dined, the householder and his wife may afterwards eat what remains.

A Brahman lady is a superlative being in the universe.

A kandala (chandaal), a village pig, a cock, a dog, a menstruating woman and a eunuch must not look at the Brahman while he is eating.

Holy rites prescribed by Vedic Text must be performed on the ceremony of conception and other sacraments by twice-born men. They sanctify the body and purify from sin in this life and after death.

Before the naval string is cut, *Gatakarmana* (birth-rite) must be performed for a male child. While sacred formulas are being recited, he must be fed honey and butter.

Not a single act here appears ever to be done by a man free from desire. For whatever a man does, it is the result of the impulse of desire.

A learned man, after fully scrutinising with the eyes of knowledge, should be intent on the performance of his duties.

The man, who obeys the law prescribed in the revealed Texts and in the sacred tradition, gains fame in this world, and after death—unsurpassable bliss.

Know that the performance of the ceremony of impregnation (Garbhadhan) is prescribed which a Brahman must perform. And, at the end of life, the funeral rites (Antyasthi) are prescribed. Sacred formulas must be recited while performing these rites.

The customs, handed down in regular succession among the castes and the mixed races of that country since time immemorial, is called the conduct of the virtuous men.

Twice-born men seek to dwell in a country where sacred knowledge prevails. But a Shudra, distressed for subsistence, seek to reside anywhere.

Let the father perform or cause to be performed the *Namadeya* (the rite of naming the child) on the tenth or twelfth day after birth, or on a lucky lunar day, in a lucky *muhurta* under an auspicious constellation.

In the fourth month, the *Nishkarmana* (the first leaving of the house) of the child should be performed. In the sixth month, the *Annaprasana* (first feeding with rice) should be performed as a custom on any auspicious day by the family.

According to the teaching of the revealed text, the *Kudakarmana* (tonsure) must be performed for the sake of spiritual merit by all twice-born men in the third year. After these periods, men of the three (castes) who have not received the sacrament at the proper time, become Vratyas (outcasts). They are excluded from the savitri (initiation) and stand despised by the Aryans.

Having taken a staff according to his choice, having worshipped the sun and walked round the fire, turning his right hand towards it, the student should beg alms according to the prescribed rule.

Let him first beg food of his mother, or of his sister, or of the own maternal aunt, or of some other female who will not disgrace him.

Having collected as much food as required, he should eat it turning his face to the east. He should purify himself by sipping water. This will procure long life if he eats facing the east. He will procure fame and prosperity if he does according to the Veda.

Let him always worship the food and eat it without contempt. When he sees it, let him rejoice. Let him show a pleased face and pray that he may always obtain it.

Food, that is always worshipped, gives strength and manly vigour. Food if eaten irreverently destroys them both. Beware of eating between the two meal-times.

He, who knows the sacred law and seeks purity, shall always perform the rite of sipping with water neither hot nor frosty.

An offering consisting of muttered prayers is ten times more efficacious than a sacrifice performed according to the rules of the Veda. A prayer which is inaudible to the ears surpasses a hundred times. The mental recitation of sacred texts surpasses a thousand times.

But undoubtedly, a Brahman reaches the highest goal by muttering prayers only, whether he performs other rites or neglects them. He, who befriends all creatures, is declared to be a true Brahman.

A wise man should strive to restrain his organs which run wild among alluring sensual objects, as a charioteer holds reign of his horse.

Through the attachment of his organs to sensual pleasure, a man doubtlessly will incur guilt. But if, he keeps them under complete control, he will obtain success in gaining his aims.

Desire is never extinguished by the enjoyment of desired objects. It only grows stronger like a fire fed with clarified butter.

If one man should obtain all these sensual enjoyments and another should renounce them all, the renunciation of all pleasures is far better than the attainment of all these.

Those organs which are strongly attached to sensual pleasure cannot so effectually be restrained by abstinence from enjoyment as by a constant pursuit of true knowledge.

Neither the study of the Veda, nor the liberty, nor sacrifice, nor any self-imposed restraint, nor austerity ever procures the attainment of rewards to a man whose heart is contaminated by sensuality.

That man may be considered to have really subdued his organs, who, on hearing, touching and seeing, on tasting and smelling anything neither rejoices nor repines.

But when, one, among all the organs, slips away from control, wisdom slips away from him.

If he keeps all the ten organs as well as the mind in subjection, he may gain all his aims without reducing his body by the practice of *yoga*.

He, who stands during the morning twilight muttering the savitri, removes the guilt collected during the previous night. But he, who recites it seated in the evening, destroys the sin he committed during the day.

But he, who does not worship standing in the morning, nor sitting in the evening, shall be excluded from all the duties and rights of an Aryan just like a Shudra.

There are no forbidden days for the daily recitation of Veda.

Unless one is asked, one must not explain anything to anybody. One must not answer a person who accepts improperly. A wise man, though he knows the answer, should behave among men, as if he were an idiot. Of the two persons, he who illegally explains anything, and he who illegally asks a question, one or both will die or incur the other's enmity.

Sacred knowledge must not be sown in students whose merit and wealth are not obtained by teaching. Such knowledge is not to be sown to him who at least does not show due obedience just as good seeds must not be thrown on barren land. Even in times of dire distress, a teacher of the Veda should rather die with his knowledge than sow it in barren soil.

He, who acquires the Veda without permission from one who recites it, incurs the guilt of stealing the Veda. He shall sink into hell.

A student shall first reverentially salute that teacher from whom he receives knowledge, referring to worldly affairs to the Veda, or to the Brahmans.

A Brahman who completely governs himself, though he knows the savitri only, is better than the Brahman who knows the three Vedas but does not control himself and eats all sorts of food and sells all sorts of goods.

He, who habitually salutes and constantly pays reverence to the aged, obtains an increase of four things, viz. length of life, knowledge, fame and strength.

A female who is the wife of another man and is not a blood relation, one must say her: "Lady Bhagavati or Beloved Sister."

The feet of the wife of one's brother (older in age), if she be of the same caste (Varna), must be clasped every day. But the feet of wives of other paternal or maternal relatives need only be embraced on one's return from a journey.

Towards a sister of one's father and of one's mother, and towards one's own elder sister, one must behave as behaving towards one's mother. But the mother is more venerable than they.

Fellow citizens are called friends.

A Shudra is worthy of honour who has entered into the tenth decade of his life.

A Sanataka and a king must be honoured. If the king and a Sanataka meet, the later receives respect from the king.

That man who truthfully fills both his ears with the Veda, the pupil shall consider him his father and mother. The pupil must never offend him.

The teacher (acharya) is ten-times more venerable than a sub-teacher (upadhyaya). The father is a hundred times more venerable than a teacher. But the mother is a thousand times more venerable than the father.

The pupil must know that a man, who benefits him by the Veda, be it little or much, is called his Guru.

A man destitute of sacred knowledge is, indeed, a child. One, who teaches him (the child) the Veda, is his father.

Greatness does not come through years. It does not come through wealth. It also does not come through powerful kinsmen. Greatness comes through learning of the Veda and acquiring knowledge of it. The sages have made this law. He, who has learnt the Veda, is considered great by us.

A man is not considered venerable because his head is gray. A man, though young but learned in the Veda, is considered to be venerable.

As a eunuch is unproductive with women, and a cow is not prolific with a cow, so as a gift made to an ignorant man yields no reward. Even so is a Brahman useless who does not know the Veda.

Created beings must be instructed in their welfare without giving them pain. Sweet and gentle speech must be used by a teacher who desires to abide by the sacred law.

Let him not (even though in pain) speak words cutting others to the quick. Let him not injure others through his words or deeds. Let him not utter speeches which make others afraid of him, since that will prevent him in gaining heaven.

An Aryan must study the whole Veda together with the *Rahasyas*. He must perform various kinds of austerities and vows at the same time prescribed by the rules of the Veda.

Let a Brahman, who desires to perform austerities, constantly repeat the Veda, for the study of the Veda, is declared to be in this world the highest austerity for a Brahman.

A student should abstain from honey, meat, perfumes, garlands and flavouring food. He must abstain from woman. A student must abstain from doing injury to living creatures.

A student must abstain from sensual desire. He must abstain from anger and covetousness. He must abstain from gambling, idle disputes, backbiting and lying. He must abstain from looking at and touching woman and from hurting others.

A student should sleep alone. Let him not waste his manhood.

A student being pure shall daily bring food from the houses of men who are not deficient in the knowledge of the Veda. He must daily bring food from houses of men who perform sacrifices and are famous for following the lawful occupation.

Let a student not beg from the relatives of his teacher. Let him not beg from his own or his mother blood relations. But if, there are no houses belonging to the strangers, he is free to beg else from.

In the presence of his teacher, let him always eat less. He should wear a lesser valuable dress and ornaments than the former. Let him rise earlier from his bed and go to rest later.

Let him not answer or converse with his teacher reclining on a bed, nor sitting, nor eating, nor slandering up if his teacher is seated. A student should stand up when his teacher stands. If the teacher advances, the student should follow him. A student should run after him when the teacher runs.

When his teacher is at rest, let his bed or seat lie below. But within sight of his teacher, he shall not sit carelessly at ease.

Let him not sit with his teacher to the ice ward or to the windward. Let him not say anything which his teacher cannot hear.

The son of a teacher, who imparts instruction in his father's behalf, whether younger or of equal age, deserves the same honour as the teacher.

A student must not shampoo the limbs of his teacher's son. A student must not assist him in bathing nor eat the fragments. The wives of the teacher, who belong to the same caste, must be treated respectfully as the teacher. But those, who belong to a different caste, must be honoured by rising and salutation.

Let him not perform for a wife of his teacher anointing her. Let him not assist her in the bath shampooing her limbs, or massaging her hair.

A pupil, who is full twenty years old and knows what is becoming and what is unbecoming, shall not salute a young wife of his teacher by clasping her feet.

A young lady shall not clasp the feet of a person of the same or about the same age.

It is the nature of women to seduce men in this world. For that reason, the wise are never unguarded in the company of females.

Women are able to lead astray in this world not only a fool but even a learned man. Women are able to make him a slave of desire and anger.

One should not sit in a lonely place with one's mother, sister or daughter, for the senses are powerful and master even a learned man.

At his pleasure, a young student may prostrate himself on the ground before the young wife of a teacher and say: Worship thee, O lady!

On returning from a journey, he must clasp the feet of his teacher's wife and salute her daily remembering the duty of the virtuous.

If a man of low caste performs anything leading to his happiness, let him diligently practise it as well as all other permitted acts in which his heart finds pleasure.

The teacher, the father, the mother and an elder brother must not be treated with disrespect, especially by a Brahman, though, one be grievously offended by them.

The teacher is the image of Brahman. The father is the image of Prajapati, the Lord of all created beings. The mother is the image of the earth. And an elder full brother is an image of ourselves.

That, trouble and pain which the parents undergo on the birth of their children cannot be compensated even in a hundred years.

Obedience towards mother, father and teacher is declared to be the best form of austerity. You must not perform any other meritorious rites without their permission.

By honouring his mother, he gains this world. By honouring his father, he gets the middle sphere. But by obedience to his teacher, he gains the world of Brahman.

All duties have been fulfilled by him who honours those three. But to him, who does not honour all them, rites performed by him remain fruitless.

He, who possesses faith, may receive learning even from a man of lower caste. The highest law must be learnt from the lowest one. And an excellent wife may be brought even from a lower family.

Even from poison, nectar may be taken. Even from a child, good advice may be taken. Even from a foe, a lesson in good conduct may be taken and even from an impure substance, the good one may be taken.

Excellent wives, learning of the knowledge of the law, the rules of purity, good advice and various sacred acts may be acquired from anybody.

It is prescribed that in times of distress, a student may learn the Veda from one who is not a Brahman. It is also prescribed that he shall work in behalf of the teacher as long as his instruction lasts.

A Brahman who does not know the Veda is unworthy. He is not better in comparison to a Shudra who never reads the Veda.

A Brahman who, thus, passes his life as a student without breaking his vow reaches after death the highest abode and will not be born again in this world.

TEACHINGS OF THE MANUSMRITI

CHAPTER III

A solemn vow of studying the Vedas must be kept under a teacher until the student has perfectly learnt them.

A student who has studied the Vedas in due order without breaking the rules of studentship shall enter the order of householders.

One who is famous for the strict performance of his duties shall be honoured.

With the permission of his teacher, a twice-born man shall marry a wife of equal caste who is endowed with auspicious marks.

Let him not marry a maiden who has reddish hair. Do not marry one who is sick. Do not marry one who has no hair on her head, nor one having too much hair on her body. Do not marry garrulous.

Do not marry a maiden named after a tree, or a river, or a mountain. Do not marry one who is named after the name of a low caste or a slave. Do not marry one whose name inspires terror.

Let him wed a female who is free from bodily defects. Marry one who has an agreeable name and who bears a graceful gait of a *hamsa* or an elephant. Marry a lady who has a moderate quantity of hair on her head and who has small teeth and soft limbs.

But a prudent man should not marry a maiden who has no brother. Do not marry one whose father is not known.

It is declared that a Shudra woman alone can be the wife of a Shudra. Twice-born men who wed wives of the low caste soon degrade their families and their children to the state of Shudras.

According to Atri and Gautama, he who weds a Shudra woman becomes an outcast. A Brahman who takes a Shudra wife to his bed will sink into hell. If he begets a child by her, he will lose the rank of a Brahman.

No father must take even the smallest amount of gratuity from his daughter. One who takes gratuity is a seller of his offspring.

A male child is produced by a greater quality of male seed. A female child is produced by the prevalence of the female.

Let the husband approach his wife in due season with a desire for conjugal union on any day excepting the *parvas*.

On the even nights, sons are conceived. On the uneven nights, daughters are conceived. Hence, a man who desires to have sons should approach his wife in due season on the even nights.

Women must be honoured and adorned by their fathers, brothers, husbands, and brothers-in-law who desire their own welfare.

A Brahman who stays one night only is declared to be a guest.

One must not consider a Brahman as a guest who dwells in the same village. Do not consider one a guest who seeks his livelihood by social intercourse.

A guest who reaches at the house in the evening must not be driven away by the householder.

Do not eat any food which you do not offer to your guest. The hospitable reception of guests procures wealth, fame, long life, and heavenly bliss.

A Kshatriya, a Vaishya or a Shudra who comes to the door of a Brahman is not a guest. Neither a personal friend nor a relative nor the teacher is a guest.

Where women are honoured, the gods are pleased. But where they are not honoured, no sacred rite yields rewards.

If the wife is radiant with beauty, the whole house is bright.

Where the female relation lives in grief, the family soon wholly perishes. But the family where the female relation is not unhappy ever prospers. Men who seek welfare should always honour women on holidays and festivals with gifts of ornaments, clothes and dainty food.

As all the creatures subsist by receiving support from air, even so the members of all orders subsist by receiving support from the householder.

A Brahman who stays unhonoured in the house takes away with him all the spiritual merit.

A Brahman shall not name his family and Vedic *gotra* in order to obtain a meal. He, who prepares food for himself alone, eats nothing but sin. It is ordained that the food which remains after the performance of the sacrifice shall be the meal of virtuous men.

Oblation to the gods and the manes must be presented by the givers to a Shrotriya alone. Whatever is given to such a worthy Brahman yields great rewards.

Let him feed at least one learned man at the sacrifice to the gods, and at least one at the sacrifice to the manes. Thus, he will gain a rich reward.

Let him make enquiry regarding the ancestors of a Brahman who has studied the entire verses of the Veda. If descended from a virtuous race, such a man is a worthy recipient of the gifts offered to the gods or to the manes.

Respect of Brahman is due to the Veda he has learnt. If lacks, he is not venerable.

Let him not entertain a personal friend at a funeral sacrifice. Let him not entertain one who maintains his affection by valuable gifts. Let him feed a Brahman at *sraddha* whom he considers neither as a foe nor as a friend.

He, who performs funeral sacrifice and offering to the gods chiefly for the sake of gaining friends, reaps after death no rewards for *sraddha* and sacrifice.

That meanest amongst twice-born man, who in his folly, connects friendship through a funeral sacrifice, loses heaven because he performed the *sraddha* for the sake of friendship.

One may also entertain on funeral sacrifices one's maternal grandfather, a maternal uncle, a sister's son, a father-in-law, one's teacher, a daughter's son, a daughter's husband, one's own officiating priest or a man for whom sacrifices are offered.

For a rite sacred to the gods, he, who knows the law, will not make too close inquiries regarding an invited Brahman. But when one performs the ceremony in honour of the manes, one must carefully examine the qualities and parentage of the guest.

Manu has declared that those Brahmans who are thieves, outcasts, eunuchs or atheist are unworthy to partake in oblation to the gods and the manes.

Let him not entertain on *sraddha* one who wears his hair in braids. Let him not entertain one who has not studied the Veda. Let him not entertain on a *sraddha* one affected with a skin disease. A gambler must not be entertained. Those must be kept away who entertain for a multitude of sacrificers.

Physicians, temple priests, sellers of men and those who subsist by shop keeping must be avoided at sacrifices offered to the gods and to the manes.

One day before the *sraddha* rite is performed, or the day when it takes place, let him invite with due respect at least three Brahmans having sacred learning.

A Brahman who has been invited to a rite in honour of the manes shall always control himself and not recite the Veda. He, who performs the *sraddha*, must act in the manner as prescribed in the sacred law.

TEACHINGS OF THE MANUSMRITI

CHAPTER IV

No guest must stay at a house without being honoured according to his ability.

Let him not honour the man who follows forbidden occupations. A Brahman should beg a king. A Brahman should beg a kshatriya. A Brahman should beg a Vaishya. But a Brahman must not beg a Shudra.

Let him not eat in the company of his wife. Let him not look at her while she eats, sneezes, yawns or sits at ease.

A Brahman who desires energy must not look at a woman who applies collyrium to her eyes. A Brahman must not look at a woman who has uncovered and opened herself.

Let one not dress with one garment. Let one not take bath naked.

One must not void urine on the road, on ashes or in the open. Do not void urine in the playground, in water, on an altar of bricks, on a mountain, or on the ruins of a temple. Do not void urine in the holes of living creatures. Do not void urine on reaching the bank of river. Do not do so on the top of a mountain.

Let him never void faeces or urine facing the wind. Never void on a fire or looking towards a Brahman, the sun, water or cows. This is the sacred learning.

Let him not sleep alone in a deserted dwelling. Let him not wake a superior who is sleeping. Let him not converse with a menstruating woman.

One must not interrupt a cow which is sucking her calf. Nor should one tell anybody of it. A wise man, if sees a rainbow in the sky, must not point it out.

One must not dwell in a village where the sacred Law is not obeyed. One must not stay long where diseases are endemic.

Let him not go alone on journey, nor reside long on a mountain. Let him not dwell in a country where the rulers are Shudra. One should not dwell in a country surrounded by unrighteous men. One should not dwell in a village swarming with the lowest castes.

One must not be a glutton. One must not eat very early in the morning. One must not exert oneself without a purpose.

Let him not eat food in his lap. Let him not show idle curiosity. One should not wash one's feet in a vessel of white brass. Let him not eat from a broken dish.

One should not use shoes, garments, a sacred string, ornaments, a garland, or a water vessel which have been used by other.

One should not go to bed with wet feet. He who eats while his feet are wet attains long life. Let him not step on hair, ashes, bones, cotton seeds or chaff if desires long life.

Let him not stay together with outcastes nor with low-caste men, nor with fools and nor with overbearing men. Let him not give advice to the Shudras. Let him not scratch his head with both hands joined. Let him not touch while he is impure.

Do not accept presents from a king who is not descended from the Kshatriya race. Do not accept presents from butcher, oil manufacturer, nor from those who subsist on the gain of prostitutes.

A king is declared to be equal in wickedness to a butcher who keeps a slaughter house. To accept presents from such a king is a terrible crime. A learned Brahman does not accept presents from such a king.

A Brahman shall not recite the Veda during these days- when he has accepted an initiation, when he is engaged in a funeral rite in honour of an ancestor and when the king has become impure through a birth or death in his family or when Rahu, by an eclipse, makes the moon impure.

Do not study Veda near a buried ground, nor do so in a cow-pen, nor dressed in a garment which you wore during conjugal intercourse.

Do not bathe immediately after a meal. Do not bathe when you are sick. Do not bathe in the middle of the night. Do not bathe in a pool which you do not know perfectly.

Do not step intentionally on the shadow of images of gods. Do not step intentionally on the shadow of a Guru, on the shadow of a king, on the shadow of a teacher or on the shadow of a reddish brown animal.

Do not step things used for cleansing the body. Do not step on urine or odour. Do not step on blood, on mucus and on anything spat out or vomited.

One must not offend the teacher. One must not offend him who explains the Veda. One must not offend cows, nor Brahmans, nor any man performing austerity. Do not offend your father, mother or Guru.

Do not raise a stick against another man. Do not strike anybody except a son or a pupil. One may beat the two slightly- the son and the pupil in order to correct them.

A wise man should never threaten a Brahman, nor strike him even with a blade of grass, nor cause his blood to flow. A Brahman must seek a means of subsistence which either causes no pain or causes at least little pain to other or live by that.

The Brahman must lead a pure, straightforward and honest life. A Brahman must avoid all means of acquiring wealth which impedes the study of the Veda.

A householder must give a Brahman as much food as he is able to spare to those who do not cook for themselves and to all beings. One must distribute food without detriment to one's own interest.

A *Sanataka* who pines with hunger, may beg wealth of a king for whom he sacrifices and of a pupil but not of others. A *Sanataka* who is able to procure food shall never waste himself with hunger. He shall not wear old or dirty clothes if he possesses property. That is a settled rule.

Do not look at the sun when it sets or rises. Do not look at the sun when it is eclipsed or reflected in water or stands in the middle of the sky.

Though mad with desire, do not approach your wife when her menstruation appears. Do not sleep with her in the same bed. The wisdom, the energy, the strength, the sight and the vitality of a man, who approaches a woman covered with menstrual secretion, utterly perish. If he avoids her while she is in that condition, his wisdom, energy, strength, sight and vitality will increase.

The intellect of a man, who voids urine against a fire, the sun, the moon in water, against the Brahman, or against the wind, perishes.

Let him not blow a fire with his mouth. Let him not look at a naked woman. Let him not throw an impure substance into the fire. And let him not warm his feet at it.

Let him not place fire under the bed. Let one not step over it. Let him not place fire at the foot or at the end of his bed when he sleeps. Let him not torment living creatures.

Let him not eat, not travel, not sleep during the twilight. Let him not scratch the ground. Let him not take off his garland. Let him not enter a walled village or a house except by the gate. And by night, let him keep at a long distance from the roots of trees.

Let him never play with dice. Let him not eat lying on the bed. Let him not eat after sunset any food containing sesame grains. Let him never sleep naked. Let him not go anywhere unpurified after meals.

Let him never enter a place difficult of access which is impervious to his eyes. Let him not look at urine or ordure. Let him not cross a river by swimming with his arms.

Let him avoid, in anger, to hold of his own or other men's hair or to strike himself or other's head.

A learned Brahman who studies the Veda and desires bliss after death does not accept presents from a king. Let him not recite the texts indistinctly. Let him not recite the Veda in the presence of Shudras.

He must not recite the Veda lying on the bed. He must not recite the Veda while his feet are raised on a bench. He must not recite the Veda while he sits with a cloth tied round his knees. Let him not study the Veda when he has eaten meat. Let him not study the Veda who has eaten food given by a person impure on account of a birth or a death.

One must not recite the Veda during a fog, nor while the sound of arrows is audible, nor during both the twilights, nor on the new moon day, nor on the fourteenth and the eighth day of each half month.

The new moon day destroys the teacher, the fourteenth day destroys the pupil, the eighth day and the full moon days destroy all remembrances of the Veda. Let him, therefore, avoid reading Vedas on these days.

A Brahman shall not recite the Veda during a dust storm. He shall not recite while the sky is prematurely red. He shall not recite the Veda while jackal howls. He shall not recite the Veda while the barking of dogs, the braying of donkeys or grunting of camels is heard. He shall not recite while he is seated in a company.

Let him not study the Veda near a buried ground, nor near a village, nor in a cow pen. Let him not recite the Veda dressed in a garment which he wore during conjugal intercourse. He must not recite the Veda present at a funeral sacrifice.

When the village has been beset with robbers, and when an alarm has been raised by fire, let him know that the Veda study must be interrupted until the same hour on the next day.

Let him not recite the Veda on horseback, nor on a tree, nor on an elephant. Let him not recite in a boat or ship. Let him not recite the Veda on a donkey or on a camel. He must not recite the Veda standing on the barren ground or riding in a carriage.

Do not recite the Veda during verbal altercation and during a mutual assault. Do not recite in a camp. Do not recite during a battle, or when you have just eaten. Do not recite the Veda during indigestion and after vomiting.

Let him not recite the Veda without receiving permission from the guest who stays in his house. Let him not recite while the wind blows vehemently, nor while blood flows from his body, nor when he is wounded by a weapon. Let him stop all Veda study for a day and night after finishing a Veda.

The Rig Veda is declared to be sacred to the gods. The Yajur Veda is declared sacred to men. And the Sama Veda is declared to be sacred to the manes.

Know that the Veda study must be interrupted for a day and a night, when cattle, a frog, a cat, a dog, a snake or a rat pass between the teacher and his pupil.

Let the twice-born man always carefully interrupt the Veda study on two occasions, viz. when the place where he recites is impure, and when he himself is not purified.

Let him not bathe immediately after a meal, nor when he is sick, nor in the middle of the night, nor dressed in all his garments. Let him not bathe in a pool which he does not perfectly know.

Let him not show particular attention to an enemy, to the friend of an enemy, to a thief and to a wicked man. Let him not show particular attention to the wife of another man. For, in this world, there is nothing such detrimental to long life as criminal conversation with another man's wife.

Never despise a learned Brahman, a Kshatriya and a snake because these three, when treated with disrespect, may utterly destroy him. Hence, a wise man must never despise them.

Let him not despise himself on account of formal failure. Until death, let him seek fortune. Be not despair of gaining it.

Let him say what is true. Let him say what is pleasing. Let him utter no disagreeable truth. And let him utter no falsehood. Let him not engage in useless enmity or dispute with anybody. That is the eternal law.

Let him not journey too early in the morning, nor too late in the evening, nor during the midday. Let him not journey alone, nor with an unknown companion, nor with Shudras.

Let him not insult those who have redundant limbs or who are deficient in limbs. Let him not insult those who are destitute of knowledge. Let him not insult those who are very aged men. Let him not insult those who have no beauty or wealth. And, let him not insult those who are of low birth.

Far from his dwelling, let him remove urine and ordure. Far from dwelling, let him remove the water used for washing his feet.

Early in the morning only, let him void faces, decorate his body, take bath, clean his teeth and apply collyrium.

On the *parva* days, let him go to visit the images of the gods and virtuous Brahman.

Let one reverentially salute venerable men who visit him. Give them your own seat. Let him sit near them with joined hands. When they leave off, accompany them walking behind.

Let him follow the conduct of virtuous men connected with his occupation.

Through virtuous conduct, he obtains long life; through virtues conduct, he obtains desirable offspring and through virtuous conduct, he obtains imperishable wealth. Virtuous conduct destroys the effect of inauspicious means.

A man of bad conduct is blamed among people. He constantly suffers misfortune. He is affected with disease. He is short-lived.

A man who follows the conduct of the virtuous is free from enemy. He lives a hundred years, though he be entirely destitute of auspicious marks.

Let him avoid all undertakings, the success of which depends on others. Let him pursue the accomplishment which depends on him.

Everything that depends on others gives pain. Everything that depends on oneself gives pleasure. Know that this is the definition of pleasure and pain.

When the performance of an act gladdens his heart, let him perform it with diligence.

Let him always delight in truthfulness (obedience) to the sacred law and conduct worthy of an Aryan. Let him chastise his pupil according to the sacred law. Let him keep his speech, his arms and his belly under control.

Let him not be uselessly active with his hands and feet, or with his eyes. Let him not talk idle. Let him not injure others by deeds or by words. Let him not even think of it.

Let him walk on that path of holy men which his fathers and his grand fathers follow. While he walks on that, he will not suffer harm.

Let him not quarrel with officiating or domestic priest, with a teacher, with a maternal uncle and with a guest. Let him not quarrel with a dependant, with infants, with aged and with sick men. Let him not quarrel with learned men and with his paternal relatives. Let one not quarrel with connexions by marriage and maternal relatives.

If he avoids all quarrels, he will be free from all sins. And by suppressing all such quarrels, a householder conquers the whole world.

The teacher is the lord of the world of Brahman. The father has power over the world of created beings. A guest rules over the world of Indra. And, the priests rule over the world of the gods.

A Brahman who neither performs austerities nor studies the Veda, yet delights in accepting gifts, sinks with the donor into hell.

Let him never bathe in a tank belonging to other men.

Let him never eat food given by intoxicated, angry or sick men. Never eat food in which hair or insects are found. Never eat food which has been touched intentionally with the foot.

Let him never eat food which the slayer of a learned Brahman has looked. Never eat food which has been touched by a menstruating woman. Never eat food which has been pecked at by birds or touched by a doe.

Let one not eat food given by a hunter and a cruel man. Let one not eat food given by a woman whose ten days of impurity have not elapsed.

Do not eat food given without due respect. Do not eat food given by a female who has no male relative. Do not eat food of an enemy, nor that given by the lord of the town, nor that given by outcast. Do not eat food on which anybody has sneezed.

Do not eat food given by an informer. Do not eat food given by one who habitually tells falsehood. Do not eat food given by an ungrateful man.

Do not eat food given by a stage player, or a dealer in weapons, or given by trainer of hunting dogs. Do not eat food given by those, who, in all matters, are ruled by women. Do not eat food given by men whose ten days of impurity on account of a death have not passed.

The food of an unchaste woman is equal to semen. And the food of a dealer in arms is as bad as dirt.

The food of a king impairs his vigour. The food of a Shudra impairs his excellence in sacred learning.

A Brahman must not eat cooked food given by a Shudra who performs no *sraddha*. He (the Brahman) may accept raw grain sufficient for one night and day.

Both, who respectfully receives a gift and one who respectfully bestows it, go to the heaven. Let him not be proud of an austerity. Let him not utter a falsehood. Let him not speak ill to Brahmans, though he is tormented by them. When one has bestowed a gift, let him not boast of it.

By falsehood a sacrifice becomes vain, and by self-complacency the reward of austerities is lost. Longevity is lost by speaking evil of Brahmans, and the reward of a gift is lost by boasting of it. Giving no pain to creatures let him accumulate spiritual merit.

For the next world, neither father, nor mother, nor sons, nor relatives stand to be companions. Spiritual merit alone remains with him.

Single is each being born; single it dies. Single it enjoys the reward of the virtue; single it suffers the punishment of its sin.

A Brahman, who always connects himself with the most excellent ones and shuns all inferior men, becomes the most distinguished. By an opposite conduct, he becomes a Shudra.

He, who describes himself to be a virtuous man in contrary to truth, is the most sinful in this world. He is a thief who makes away with his own self.

TEACHINGS OF THE MANUSMRITI

CHAPTER V

One should carefully avoid the milk of a cow or other female animal within ten days of her calving. Carefully avoid the milk of a cow that has no calf with her.

A Brahman must never eat the flesh of animals. One must shun the meat. Meat can never be obtained without injury to living creatures. And injury to living beings is detrimental to him. It is an obstacle in attainment of heavenly bliss.

One should entirely abstain from eating flesh. He, who does not eat meat, is dear to men and he will not be tormented by disease.

He, who permits the slaughter of an animal, he who cuts it up, he who kills it, he who buys or sells meat, he who cooks it, he who serves, and he who eats it, must also be considered as the slayers of the animal.

There is no sin in eating meat. There is no sin in taking spirituous liquor. There is no sin in carnal intercourse because it is the natural way of created beings. But abstention from all these brings great rewards.

A woman is purified by a miscarriage after conception for natural reason. A menstruating woman becomes pure by bathing after the menstrual secretion has ceased to flow.

If death happens, a Brahman shall remain impure only until the first period of ten days. A Brahman shall be pure after ten days, a Kshatriya shall be pure after twelve days, a Vaishya shall be pure after fifteen days. But a Shudra is purified after a month.

A king is the incarnation of the eight guardian deities of the world—the moon, the fire, the sun, the wind, Indra, (the Lord of water, Kubera and Varuna (Lord of wealth) and Yama.

Let him not allow a dead Brahman to be carried out by a Shudra, when men of the same caste are present. That, burnt offering, which is defiled by a Shudra's touch, is detrimental to the deceased's passage to heaven.

A river is purified by its current. A woman whose thoughts have been impure is purified by the menstrual secretion. And, a Brahman is purified by doing good to the world.

The body is cleansed by water. The internal organ is purified by truthfulness. The individual soul is purified by sacred learning and austerities. The intellect is purified by knowledge.

An earthen vessel which has been defiled by spirituous liquor, urine, odour, saliva, pus or blood cannot be purified either by burning or by any means.

Land is purified by five modes, viz. by sweeping, by smearing it with cowdung, by sprinkling it with cow's urine, by scrapping and by cows staying on it during a day and night.

The hand of an artisan is always pure. Every vendible commodity exposed for sale in the market is always pure. Food obtained by begging which a student holds in his hand is always fit for use. This is a settled law.

The mouth of a woman is always pure. The mouth of a bird is always pure when it causes a fruit to fall. The mouth of a calf is pure on the flowing of the milk.

Manu has declared that the flesh of an animal killed by deer is pure. Likewise, a beast slain by carnivorous animals or by men of low caste (dalits) is pure.

Drops of clean water, a shadow, a cow, a horse, the rays of the sun, dust, earth, the wind and fire—one must know to pure to the touch.

Oily exudations, semen, blood, brain, urine, faeces, the mucus of the nose, ear-wax, phlegm, tears, the rheum of the eyes and sweat—are the twelve impurities of human bodies.

By a girl, by a young woman or even by an aged one (woman), nothing must be done all independently, even in her own house. In childhood, a female must be subject to her father. In youth, she must be subject to her husband. And when her lord (husband) is dead, she must be subject to her son. A woman must never be alone.

She must not seek to separate herself from her father, from her husband, or from her sons. By leaving those, she would make both her own and her husband's families contemptible.

A woman must always be cheerful. She must be clever in the management of her household affairs. She must be careful in cleaning her utensils. And, she must be economical in expenditure.

She, who co-habits with a man of higher caste, forsaking her own husband who belongs to a lower one, will become contemptible in the world, and is called a remarried woman.

By violating her duty towards her husband, a wife is disgraced in this world. After death, she enters the womb of a jackal, and is tormented by disease (the punishment of her sin).

A woman controlling her thoughts, words, and deeds never slights her lord. She resides after death with her husband in heaven and is called a virtuous.

He who eats fish is an eater of every kind of flesh. A twice-born man who knowingly eats mushrooms, a village pig, garlic, a village cock, onion becomes an outcast.

A twice-born man of virtuous disposition, whether he dwells in his house, whether he dwells with a teacher, or whether he dwells in the forest, must never cause an injury to any creature.

A child that had died before the completion of its second year, the relative shall carry out of the village decked with flowers and bury it in pure ground without collecting the bones afterwards. Such a child shall not be burnt with fire, and libation of water shall be offered to it. Leave it like a log of wood in the forest. The relative shall remain impure during three days only. Let the relative eat food without factitious salt. Let him abstain from meat, and sleep separate on the ground.

When a fellow student dies, impurity is for one day. When a teacher dies, the impurity is due for three days. When a teacher's son or wife dies, impurity lasts for a day and a night. That is a settled rule.

Outcast marriage is sure to bring pain, grief or distress to the family.

No sacrifice, no fast and no vow must be performed by women apart from their husbands. If a wife obeys her husband, she will be exalted in heaven. A faithful wife, who desires to dwell will her husband, must never do anything that might displeases him who took her hand.

A virtuous wife after the death of her husband constantly remains chaste and reaches heaven, though she has no son.

TEACHINGS OF THE MANUSMRITI

CHAPTER VI

When a householder sees his skin wrinkled and hair white, and when he sees the sons of his sons, then he may resort to the forest. He should abandon all his belongings. He may depart into the forest, either leaving his wife to his sons, or accompanied by her.

Let him always be industrious in privately reciting the Veda. Let him be patient on hardships. Be ever liberal. Never be a receiver of gifts. Be compassionate towards all living creatures. Let him eat vegetables that grow on dry land or in water. Let him eat flowers, roots and fruits. Let him avoid honey, flesh and mushrooms.

A man having got rid of his body by one of those modes that are practiced by the great sages is exalted in the world of Brahman. He is free from sorrow and fear.

If he has passed the third part of natural term of his life, he may live as an ascetic during the fourth part of his existence. He should abandon all attachment to worldly objects. He who subdues his senses after offering sacrifices gains bliss after death.

Having studied the Vedas in accordance with the rule, having begotten sins according to the Sacred Law, and having offered sacrifices according to his ability, he may direct his mind to the attainment of final liberation.

Let him wonder alone without any companion in order to attain final liberation. He shall neither possess a fire, nor a dwelling. He may go to a village for his food. He shall be indifferent to everything. He shall be firm in purpose. He shall be meditating and concentrating his mind on Brahman.

Let him not desire to die. Let him not desire to live. Let him wait for his appointed time as a servant waits for the payment of his wages.

Let him keep his heart pure. Let him patiently bear hard words. Let him not insult anybody. And, let him not become anybody's enemy for the sake of this perishable body.

Against an angry man, let him not show anger. Let him bless when he is cursed. Let him not utter speech devoid of the truth.

Let him go near a house filled with hermits, Brahmans, birds, dogs or other mendicants. His vessels shall not be made of metal. His vessels shall be free from fractures.

Let him go to beg. Let him not be eager to obtain a large quantity. An ascetic who eagerly seeks alms attaches himself also to sensual enjoyment.

Let him not be sorry when he obtains nothing. Let him not rejoice when he obtains something. Let him accept so much only as it will be necessary to sustain life.

Be eating little. Be standing and sitting in solitude. Let him restrain his senses if they are attracted by sensual objects.

By the restraint of his senses, by the destruction of hatred, and by the abstention from injuring the creatures, he becomes fit for immortality.

He, who possesses the true insight into the nature of the world, is not fettered by his deeds. But he who is destitute of that insight is drawn into the circle of births and deaths.

In order to preserve living creatures, let him walk carefully scanning the ground. A twice-born man, who becomes an ascetic, shakes off his sins and reaches the highest Brahman.

Contentment, forgiveness, self-control, abstention from unrighteously appropriating anything, obedience to the rules of purification, coercion of the organs, wisdom, knowledge of the supreme soul, truthfulness, and abstention from anger are the tenfold Law.

Those Brahmans who thoroughly study the tenfold Law, and after studying obey it, enter the highest state.

Having given up the performance of all rites, throwing off the guilt of his sinful acts, subduing his organs and having studied the Veda, he may live at ease under the protection of his sons. Above is the law for self-restrained ascetics.

TEACHINGS OF THE MANUSMRITI

CHAPTER VII

The Lord created a king for the protection of this whole creation. A king has been formed of particles of lords. He, therefore, surpasses all created beings in lustre. Like the sun, he burns and heats. No one can gaze at him.

A king is a supernatural power. He is fire and wind. He is the sun and the moon. He is the Lord of Justice (Yama). He is *Kubera*. He is *Varuna,* and he is the great *Indra*. Even an infant king must not be despised from an idea that he is a mere mortal, for he is a great deity in human form.

Fire burns one man only if he carelessly approaches it. But the fire of a king's anger consumes the whole family together with its cattle and hoard of property. The man, who in his exceeding folly hates him, will doubtlessly perish, for the king quickly makes up his mind to destroy such a man.

Punishment alone governs all created beings. Punishment does protect them. If punishment is properly inflicted after due consideration, it makes all people happy. But if inflicted without considerations, it destroys everything.

The whole world is kept in order by punishment. A guiltless man is hard to find. Through fear of punishment, the whole world yields the enjoyment. If the king does not inflict the punishment, the stronger would roast the weaker like fish on a pit.

All castes (Varnas) would be corrupted by inter-mixture. Hence, no inter-caste marriage allowed.

All barriers would be broken through, and all men would rage against each other in consequence of mistakes with respect to punishment.

Punishment possesses a very bright lustre. It is hard to be administered by men with unimproved minds. It strikes down the king who swerves from his duty together with his relatives.

Punishment cannot be inflicted justly by one who has no assistant. It cannot be administered by a fool, not it can be given by a covetous man.

Punishment cannot be given by one whose mind is unimproved, not by one who is addicted to sensual pleasure.

The king has been created to be the protector of the castes (Varnas) and orders. All, according to their rank, discharge their duties. A Kshatriya, who has received, according to the rule, the sacrament prescribed by the Veda, must duly protect this whole world.

The king should rise early in the morning. The kind should worship Brahmans who are well versed in the threefold sacred science and learned in polity. The king must follow their advice.

The king is not to turn back in battle in order to protect the people and to keep to the honour. The king, who seeks to slay in battle, who fights with the utmost exertion and who does not turn back, goes to heaven.

The Brahman is the best means for a king to secure happiness.

A Kshatriya, who has received order to rule the sacraments, must duly protect the whole world. The highest duty of a Kshatriya is to protect his subjects. Let no man transgress the Law.

When he fights with the foes in battle, let him not strike with weapon concealed in the wood. Let him not strike one, who in fear climbed an eminence. Let him not strike a eunuch, not one who raises the palms of his hands in supplication. Let him not strike one who flees with flying hair, not one who sits down. Let him not strike one who says: "I am thine."

In the battle, do not strike one who sleeps. Do not strike one who has lost his court of mail. Do not strike one who is naked, not one who is disarmed, not one who looks down without taking part in battle, not one who is fighting with another foe.

Do not strike one whose weapons are broken. Do not strike one afflicted with sorrow, not one who has been grievously wounded. Do not strike one who is in fear, not one who has turned to flight. But in all these cases, let him remember the duties of the honourable warriors.

His enemy must not know his weakness, but he must know the weakness of the enemy. As a tortoise hides its limbs, even so, let him secure the members of his government against treachery. Let him protect his own weak points.

The monarch, whose subjects are carried off by the robber from his kingdom, and while carrying they are loudly calling for help, but his servants are quietly looking on it, is a dead and not a living king.

A king who is in good health must observe the rules of the Law. But if he is indisposed, he may entrust all his business to his servants.

TEACHINGS OF THE MANUSMRITI

CHAPTER VIII

A king desirous of investigating Law cases must enter his Court of Justice preserving a dignified demeanour together with Brahmans and well experienced councillors.

A Brahman who subsists only by the name of his caste or one who merely causes himself a Brahman, though his origin be uncertain, may at the king's pleasure, interpret the Law to him. But a Shudra can never interpret the Law.

Woman should give evidence for woman. Shudra can give evidence for a Shudra. And men at the lowest caste should give evidence for the lowest.

A witness, who speaks the truth in his evidence, gains after death the most excellent regime of bliss.

He, who gives false evidence, is firmly bound by Varuna's fetters. He remains helpless during one hundred existences. Let men, therefore, give true evidence.

By truthfulness, a witness is purified. Through truthfulness, his merit grows. Truth must be spoken by witnesses of all castes (Varnas).

Whenever the death of a Shudra, the death of a Vaishya, the death of a Kshatriya or the death of a Brahman would be caused by a declaration of the truth, false may be spoken because such falsehood is preferable to the truth.

Let no wise man swear an oath falsely even in a thrift matter. He, who swears an oath falsely, is lost in this world and after death.

A Kshatriya having defamed a Brahman shall be fined one hundred Panas. A Vaishya having defamed a Brahman shall be fined one hundred and fifty or two hundred. A Shudra shall suffer corporeal punishment.

A Brahman shall be fined fifty Panas for defaming a kshatriya. In the case of a Vaishya defaming a Kshatriya, the fine shall be twenty five and in the case of a Shudra defaming a Kshatriya, the fine shall be twelve panas.

A once-born man (Shudra) who insults a twice-born man with gross invective shall have his tongue cut out, for he is of low origin.

If a Shudra mentions his name and caste as a twice-born, an iron nail ten fingers long shall be thrust red hot into his mouth.

If a Shudra arrogantly teaches Brahmans their duty, the king shall cause hot oil to be poured into his mouth and into his ears.

With whatever limb a man of a low caste does hurt to a man of the three highest castes even that limbs shall be cut off. That is the teaching of the great Manu.

He, who raises his hand or a stick, shall have his hand cut off. He, who in anger kicks with his foot, shall have his foot cut off.

A low caste man, who tries to place himself on the same seat with a man of a high caste, shall be bounded on his hip and be banished, or the king shall cause his buttock to be gashed.

If out of arrogance, he spits on a superior, the king shall cause both his lips to be cut off. If he passes urine on him, the penis shall be cut out. If he breaks wind/emits foul gas against him, the anus shall stand cut off.

If he lays hold of the heir of a superior, let the king unhesitatingly cut off his hands.

A wife, a son, a slave, a pupil and a younger brother of the full blood who have committed faults, may be beaten with a rope or a split bamboo.

The king is ever worthy of honour who ensures the safety of the subjects.

Know that a king who heeds not the rules of the Law, who is an atheist and rapacious and who does not protect his subjects but devours will sink low after death. A king who desires his own welfare must always sacrifice litigates, infants, and sick men, who inveigh against him.

Neither a father, nor a teacher, nor a friend, nor a mother, nor a wife, nor a son and nor a domestic priest must be left unpunished by a king if they do not keep within their duty.

In case of a theft, the guilt of a Shudra shall be eightfold. In case of a theft, the guilt of a Vaishya shall be sixteenfold. And in case of a theft, the guilt of a Kshatriya shall be thirty-twofold. Know that in case of a theft, the guilt of a Brahman shall be sixty-fourfold or quite a hundredfold, knowing the nature of the offence.

One may slay without hesitation an assassin who approaches with murderous intent, whether he is one's teacher, a child, an aged man or a Brahman deeply vested in the Vedas. By killing an assassin, the slayer incurs no guilt whether he does it publically or secretly. In that, fury recoils upon fury.

Let no man converse with the woman of twice-born caste (Varna) guarded or unguarded. He shall be punished in the following manner:

If she was unguarded, he will lose the art of offending and all his property. If she was guarded, he will lose everything even his life.

For intercourse with a guarded Brahmin, a Vaishya shall forfeit all his property after imprisonment for a year. For intercourse with a guarded Brahmin, a Kshatriya shall be fined one thousand Panas and he shall be shaved with the urine of an ass.

If a Vaishya or a Kshatriya has connection with an unguarded Brahmin, let him fine the Vaishya five hundred Panas and the Kshatriya one thousand. If they offered with a Brahmin or with the wife of an eminent man, they shall be punished like a Shudra, or be burnt in a fire of dry grass.

Let him never slay a Brahman, though he has committed all possible crimes. Let him banish such an offender leaving all his property to him and his body unhurt.

No greater crime is known on the earth than slaying a Brahman. A king, therefore, must not even conceive in his mind the thought of killing a Brahman.

A Brahman shall be compelled to pay a fine of one thousand Panas if he has intercourse with guarded female of those two castes.

A Brahman who approaches females of the Kshatriya or Vaishya caste, his fine shall be fixed for five hundred (panas). But for the intercourse with a female of the lowest caste, fine shall be one thousand.

A blind man, an idiot, a cripple—who moves with the help of a board, and a man full seventy years old, shall not be compelled by a king to pay tax.

A woman who has been pregnant for two months or more, a hermit in a forest, and Brahmans who are students of the Veda shall not be made to pay toll at ferry.

A wife, a son and a slave—these three are declared to have no property. The wealth they earn is acquired for him to whom they belong.

A Brahman may confidently seize the goods of the Shudra (slave), for that slave can have no property. His master may take his all possessions.

TEACHINGS OF THE MANUSMRITI

CHAPTER IX

A woman must be kept in truthful dependence by the males of her family. Her father protects her in childhood. Her husband protects her in youth and her sons protect her in old age. A woman is never fit for blind independence. Women must particularly be guarded against evil inclinations. If they are not interested, they will bring sorrow on the two families. He, who carefully guards his wife, preserves the purity of his offspring and virtuous conduct of his family. No man can completely guard a woman by force.

A Brahman wife may be superseded in the eighth year of her marriage, if gives no birth to a child. She whose children die in the tenth may be superseded. She who bears only daughters and no son may be superseded in the eleventh year. But she who is quarrelsome must be superseded without delay.

The property of a Brahman must never be taken by the king. That is a settled rule. But the property of men of other castes, the king may take in failure of all heirs.

Varuna is the lord of punishment. He holds the sceptre even over kings. A Brahman who has learnt the whole Veda is the lord of the whole world.

TEACHINGS OF THE MANUSMRITI

CHAPTER X

Let the three castes (Varnas) discharge their duties. Let them study the Vedas. But among them, the Brahman shall teach it. The other two castes shall not teach. That is an established rule.

The Brahman must know the means of subsistence prescribed by Law for all. Let him instruct others and live according to the Law.

On account of his pre-eminence, on account of the superiority of his origin, on account of the observance of restrictive rules, and on account of his particular sanctification, the Brahman is the lord of all castes (Varnas).

The Brahman, the Kshatriya, and the Vaishya (castes) are the twice-born ones. But the fourth Varna, i.e. the Shudra, has one birth only. There is no fifth caste.

In case a man of low caste, who through covetousness, lives by the occupation of a higher one, the king shall deprive him of his property and banish. He, who lives accordingly to the Law of another caste, is instantly excluded from his own caste.

A Shudra cannot commit an offence causing loss of caste. He is not worth to receive in sacraments. He has no right to fulfil the sacred laws of the Aaryans. Shudras, who are desirous to gain merit and know their duty commit no sin, but gain all praise.

The more a Shudra, keeping himself free from envy, imitates the behaviour of the virtuous, the more he gains without being censured this world and the next.

No collection of wealth must be made by a Shudra, even though he is able to do so, because a Shudra who has acquired wealth gives pain to Brahman.

A base born man resembles in character his father or his mother or both. He can never conceal his real nature.

Abstention from injuring creatures, abstention from unlawfully appropriating the goods of others, purity and control of organs—Manu has declared this to be the summary of the Law for the four Varnas.

If a female of the caste of Brahman and a Shudra female bear children to one of the highest caste, the inferior attains the highest caste within the seventh generation.

A Vaishya who is unable to subsist by his own duties may even maintain himself by a Shudra's mode of life avoiding acts forbidden to him. But he should give it up when he is able to do so.

A Kshatriya who, in times of distress, takes even the fourth part of the crops is free from guilt if he protects his subjects to the best of his ability.

His peculiar duty is conquest. He must not turn back in danger. Having protected the Vaishya by his weapon, he may cause the legal tax to be collected.

TEACHINGS OF THE MANUSMRITI

CHAPTER XI

A Brahman shall never beg for a Shudra's property for a sacrifice. A Brahman who, havingbegged for any property for a sacrifice, does not use the whole for that purpose becomes a vulture for a hundred years.

A Brahman who knows the Law need not bring any offence to the notice of the king. By his own power alone, he can punish these men who injure him. The power of a Brahman is greater than the power of a king. The Brahman, therefore, may punish his foes by his own power alone. The Brahman is declared to be the creator of the world. He is the punisher, the teacher and a benefactor of all created beings.

Neither a girl, nor a married young woman, nor a man of little learning, nor a fool, nor a man in great suffering shall offer an Agnihotra, for such persons offering an oblation sink into hell as well as he to whom that Agnihotra belongs. Hence, the person who sacrifices for another must be skilled in the performance of rites, and must know the whole Veda.

He, who drinks unintentionally the spirituous liquor, becomes pure by being initiated again. For drinking it intentionally, a penalty restrictive to life must be imposed. That is a settle rule.

The pursuit of sacred knowledge is the austerity of a Brahman. Protecting the people is the austerity of a Kshatriya. The pursuit of his daily business is the austerity of a Vaishya. And, service is the pursuit of the austerity of a Shudra.

One should give, according to one's ability, wealth to Brahmans learned in the Veda. Thus, one obtains after death heavenly bliss.

A Kshatriya must never take the property of a virtuous Brahman. But he, who is starving, may appropriate the possessions of a dasyu. A Kshatriya may take the property of one who neglects his sacred duties.

A stealer of a lamp will become blind.

Carnal intercourse with females of lower caste is prohibited.

The Brahman is declared to be the root to the sacred Law. The Kshatriya is declared to be the top of the sacred Law. Hence, he, who has confessed the sin before the assembly of such men, becomes pure.

By his origin alone, a Brahman is a deity even for the gods. His teaching is authoritative for men because the Veda is the foundation for that.

He, who violates the Guru's bed, shall, after confessing his crime, extend himself on a heated iron bed or embrace the red hot image of a woman. By dying, he becomes pure.

When a cow is sick, or is threatened by danger from thieves, tiger and the like, or falls in a morass, he must relieve her by all possible means.

In heat, in rain, or in cold, or when the wind blows violently, he must not seek to shelter himself without first sheltering the cows according to his ability.

Let him not say a word, if a cow eats anything in his own or another's house, or field, or on the threshing floor. Let him not say a word if a calf drinks milk.

He, who desires to be pure, must not eat forbidden food. He must vomit up such as he has eaten unintentionally or quickly atone for it by various means of purification.

TEACHINGS OF THE MANUSMRITI

CHAPTER XII

That man who keeps control over himself with respect to all created beings and wholly subdues his desire and wrath gains complete success.

Goodness is declared to have the form of knowledge. Darkness is declared to have the form of ignorance and hatred.

The slayer of a Brahman exerts the wombs of a dog, a pig, an ass, a camel, a crow, a goat, a sheep, a deer and a bird.

A Brahman who drinks the spirituous liquor called *Sura* shall enter the bodies of snakes and large insects. He shall enter the body of moths and birds.

A Brahman who steals the gold of a Brahman shall pass a thousand times through the bodies of spiders, snakes, lizards and of aquatic animals.

The four castes, the three worlds, the four orders, the past, the present, and the future are all severely known by means of the Veda.

The eternal lore of the Veda upholds all created beings.

Command of armies, royal authority, the office of a judge, and sovereignty over the whole world—he determines who knows the Veda science.

Austerity and sacred learning are the best means by which a Brahman secures supreme bliss. By austerities, he destroys guilt. By sacred learning, he obtains the cessation of births and deaths. A twice-born man who recites his laws revealed by Manu will be always virtuous in conduct and will reach whatever condition he desires.

Actions that spring from the mind, actions that spring from speech and actions that spring from the body produce either good or bad results. By actions are caused the various conditions of men—of the highest, of the middling and of the lowest.

6

CONCLUSION

The Manusmriti projects an ideal society. It projects an ideal human conduct. It gives an ideal look to establish an orderly society. It teaches us to lead a divine centred and happy life. It provides a base for the rulers to enforce lawful conduct. Its purpose is to inculcate discipline in people.

The Manusmriti gives the learning of virtues like compassion, forbearance, faithfulness, non-injury, self-control, non-desiring, meditation, serenity, sweetness and honesty which every person must learn and practise.

To promote these ideals and enforce divine will, it proposes numerous laws to minutely govern human life and conduct as applicable to their social classes, duties and responsibilities.

Though, some of the teachings given in the Manusmriti seem to have little bearing with the present day situation, it has not lost its importance in the eyes of the mass civil society. They still read, learn and obey. They even worship this book like the Vedas and the Gita with same sanctification.

People in a civil society should read this book, comply with its teachings and obey its orders at their discretion.